Jack
and Jill

Illustrated by Laura Huliska-Beith

Designed by Jaime Lucero

ISBN: 978-0-545-26770-0

Copyright © 2010 by Scholastic Inc.

12 11 10 9 8 7 6 5 4 3 2 1   10 11 12 13 14 15/0

Jack and Jill

went up the hill

4 to fetch

a pail of water.

Jack fell down

and broke his crown,

and Jill came tumbling after.